High-Interest/ Low-Readability

The Fairy Tale Times

Ten Fairy Tales Rewritten as High-Interest Front Page News Articles with Comprehension Activities and Audio CD

by
Sherrill B. Flora
and
Jo Browning-Wroe

illustrated by
Julie Anderson

Publisher
Key Education Publishing Company, LLC
Minneapolis, Minnesota

CONGRATULATIONS ON YOUR PURCHASE OF A KEY EDUCATION PRODUCT!

The editors at Key Education are former teachers who bring experience, enthusiasm, and quality to each and every product. Thousands of teachers have looked to the staff at Key Education for new and innovative resources to make their work more enjoyable and rewarding. Key Education is committed to developing and publishing educational materials that will assist teachers in building a strong and developmentally appropriate curriculum for young children.

PLAN FOR GREAT TEACHING EXPERIENCES WHEN YOU USE
EDUCATIONAL MATERIALS FROM KEY EDUCATION PUBLISHING COMPANY, LLC

Credits
Authors: Sherrill B. Flora and
Jo Browning-Wroe
Art Director: Annette Hollister-Papp
Illustrator: Janet Armbrust
Editor: George C. Flora
Production: Key Education Staff
Broadcaster on Audio CD:
George and Sherrill Flora

Key Education welcomes manuscripts
and product ideas from teachers.
For a copy of our submission guidelines,
please send a self-addressed,
stamped envelope to:
Key Education Publishing Company, LLC
Acquisitions Department
9601 Newton Avenue South
Minneapolis, Minnesota 55431

About the Author of the Stories:

Jo Browning Wroe has taught both in the United Kingdom and in the United States. She earned her undergraduate degrees in English and Education from Cambridge University, Cambridge, England. She worked for twelve years in educational publishing before completing a Masters Degree in Creative Writing from the University of East Anglia, Norwich, England. Most of her time is now spent writing teacher resource materials and running workshops for others who love to write. Jo has been the recipient of the National Toy Libraries Award. She lives in Cambridge, England with her two daughters, Alice and Ruby, and her husband, John.

About the Author of the Activities:

Sherrill B. Flora is the Publisher of Key Education. Sherrill earned her undergraduate degrees in Special Education and Child Psychology from Augustana College and a Masters Degree in Educational Administration from Nova University. Sherrill spent ten years as a special education teacher in the inner city of Minneapolis before beginning her twenty-year career in educational publishing. Sherrill has authored over 100 teacher resource books, as well as hundreds of other educational games and classroom teaching aids. She has been the recipient of three Director's Choice Awards, three Parent's Choice Awards, and a Teacher's Choice Award. She lives in Minneapolis, Minnesota with her two daughters, Katie and Kassie, and her very supportive husband, George.

Standard Book Number: 1-933052-30-9
High-Interest/Low Readability:
The Fairy Tale Times
Copyright © 2006 by Key Education Publishing Company, LLC
Minneapolis, Minnesota 55431

Introduction

About the Stories

The stories and activities found in *High Interest/Low Readability: The Fairy Tale Times* have been specifically designed for students who are reading below grade level; for students who have reading disabilities; and for students who are reluctant or discouraged readers.

The engaging stories are written between early-first grade and early-third grade reading levels. Each story's specific reading level and word count can be found above the story title on the Table of Contents (page 4). This information should help guide the teacher in choosing stories that are appropriate for the individual needs of the students. *(Reading grade levels are not printed on any of the stories or on any of the reproducible activity pages.)*

The stories were created with large print. Struggling readers are often intimidated and easily overwhelmed by small print. The easy-to-read large font, picture clues, and sentence structure should help children feel more confident as they read the stories included in *The Fairy Tale Times* news articles.

All the stories use high-frequency words and essential vocabulary. A list of the story's high-frequency words, as well as the special words that are necessary for each story, are found on pages 61 and 62. Prior to reading a story, review the word lists and introduce and practice any unfamiliar words. Make flash cards of the new words and outline each letter with glitter glue to provide a tactile experience for the students. Draw a picture of the word on each card to help students visualize any new vocabulary.

About the Audio CD: "The Fairy Tale Times Evening News"

Each story comes with its own evening news broadcast and begins with a few seconds of introductory music. Following the music, the news anchor welcomes the listeners and says, "Tonight's headline story is. . .. " That is the student's clue to listen. The news anchor reads the headline title and the content of the story exactly as it is printed on the student's copy of the news article.

For many struggling readers, being able to listen to the story first can be extremely beneficial. Knowing the story's content ahead of time provides students with the opportunity of using context clues to help decode words and for interpreting the meaning of the story. For other students, being able to track the text as they listen to the words allows for a beneficial multi-sensory experience. Students can hear the words; see the words; and can touch each word as they follow along listening to the evening news broadcast.

About the Activity Pages

Paper and pencil tasks are often "not fun" for struggling readers. The majority of the reproducible activity pages are divided into two different activities per page. The teacher may choose to assign both halves at once. The diversity of the two different activities should encourage the children to finish the page and not become bored or frustrated. The teacher may also choose to cut the page in two and assign each half at different times.

Coloring, drawing, solving puzzles, and cutting and pasting activities have been included. These types of activities reinforce a wide range of reading skills and are often viewed as "more fun" by the students.

In short, *High Interest/Low Readability: The Fairy Tale Times* will provide your students with a complete reading experience.

Contents

Big Bad Wolf in Hospital

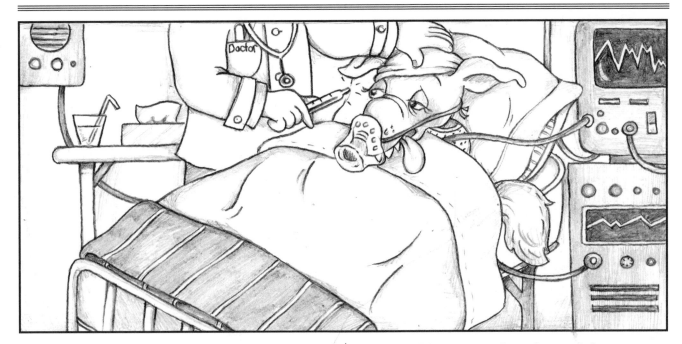

The Big Bad Wolf must stop huffing and puffing. He needs to rest. The doctors will keep him in the hospital.

Paul Pig's brick house was too much for Wolf. He huffed and puffed all day. He just could not blow it down. Now he will be in the hospital for a week.

Pigs all over the land have gone out to buy bricks. Most stores have run out.

"It was too easy for Wolf to blow down my brothers' houses," said Paul Pig. "The days of straw and sticks are over. If Wolf visits any pig in this land, he will need more than a huff and a puff!"

Name_____

Directions: Choose the correct word from the Word Bank to complete each sentence.

> **Word Bank:**   bricks   week   hospital   huffing   puffing

1. The wolf is in the _____ .

2. The pigs all want to buy _____ .

3. The Wolf will be in the hospital for a _____ .

4. The Wolf must stop_____ and _____ .

5. Do you think pigs will build with straw and sticks again?

   Why or why not?_____

   _____

Directions: Pretend you own a store that sells bricks. Create an advertisement for your store that can be printed in *The Fairy Tale Times* newspaper.

Name_____

Directions: Look at the pictures at the bottom of the page.
Cut them out along the dotted lines and glue them in sequential order.

1	2
3	4

-7- *The Fairy Tale Times*

The Fairy Tale Times

Human in Bears' Home

Mr. and Mrs. Bear said their walk in the woods ended badly.

Mrs. Bear said, "We came home to find the house in a mess. Food eaten, chairs broken."

But this was not all! They were in for an even bigger shock. The human was still in the house! When Mr. Bear went upstairs, there she was, asleep in his son's bed.

Police say that all bears should lock up their homes if they take a walk. The human girl may still be hiding in the woods.

Bruno, aged 4, was too upset to speak to The Fairy Tale Times. "He is very upset," said Mrs. Bear, "She ate his porridge. She broke his chair. She slept in his bed."

Mrs. Bear went on to say, "It will be a long time before he sleeps in that bed again. I will clean the whole house today. Those golden hairs are all over the place."

Name _____

Directions: This is the home of the Three Bears. Read each question and then color the picture in the house that answers the question.

1. Find what the human girl ate and color it yellow.
2. Find what the human girl broke and color it red.
3. Find where the human girl is hiding and color her.
4. Find Bruno's bed and color it blue.
5. Find the lock on the door and color it purple.
6. Mrs. Bear is going to clean. Find and color her broom brown.

Name _____

Directions: Choose the correct word from the Word Bank to complete each sentence.

| **Word Bank:** woods | chair | porridge | mess | hairs | talk |

1. Bruno Bear's _____ was all gone!

2. Bruno Bear's _____ was broken!

3. There were golden _____ all over the place!

4. Bruno Bear would not _____ to The Fairy Tale Times!

5. The whole house was a _____ !

6. The girl might still be hiding in the _____ !

Creative Writing

Directions: Draw a picture of the Three Bears and write a sentence about them.

Needed! Frogs to Kiss

Frog fever grips the land! A talking frog spoke to the Princess. Her golden ball had fallen into the well. The frog said he could get it out. But first, she **would have to kiss him.**

The Princess did not want to kiss the frog. But she did and now she is so happy. He turned into a prince.

Now, there just are not enough frogs in the land! All the women want their very own frog.

This morning, a woman told The Fairy Tale Times a scary story. Last night when she kissed her husband good night, he turned into a frog!

We have tried to talk with the husband. But now that he is a real frog, all he can say is, "Ribbit."

Police Frog Fred said, "Frogs have never had it so good! Every woman wants to kiss a frog." Police Frog Fred told all the frogs to go to the kissing booth. "Wait in line for your kiss."

"I am a real Princess," said the Princess, "I am not sure that any old kiss will turn a frog into a prince."

Name _____

Directions: Cut out the frog puzzle pieces and glue them together in the box.

Name_____

Directions: Read the question in each box. Write your answer in each speech bubble.

1. What do you think the talking frog is saying to the Princess?

2. What do you think the Police Frog is saying to the other frogs?

3. What do you think the girl is saying to the frog?

4. What do you think the woman is screaming about?

Name_____

Directions: Write an advertising slogan on the front of the kissing booth.
Color the picture.

The Fairy Tale Times

King's Horses and Men Fail to Put Humpty Dumpty Together

Three days after the fall of Humpty Dumpty, the poor egg was still not back together. He was still in pieces all over the palace garden. The King's Army worked hard to fix him. They just could not do it!

The friendly egg loved to sit on the palace wall. He would smile and wave at the children. Humpty Dumpty will be sadly missed.

At noon, the Queen stomped out of the palace. She said to the King, "You silly man! Horses are no good at fixing tiny things. Their hooves are too big. And we all know that your men are not very good at mending things."

So, the King's horses and the King's men stopped work. The Queen's women jumped in and started working. They were very good at mending. The women had Humpty Dumpty back up on the wall, in one piece, before tea.

"It is not as easy as you think," said a soldier. "Humpty was a very big egg. His shell broke into hundreds of pieces. Do not fear. All the King's horses and all the King's men are working hard. We just need more time."

Name _____

Directions: Read each sentence about the story. Write a "**T**" on the blank if the sentence is true. Write an "**F**" on the blank if the sentence is false.

1. The King's horses and men worked for 7 days to put Humpty Dumpty back together again. _____

2. Humpty Dumpty loved to sit on the palace wall and wave to the children. _____

3. Humpty's shell broke into hundreds of pieces. _____

4. Horses are good at mending things. _____

5. The women were good at puzzles and stitching. _____

6. The women had Humpty Dumpty fixed and back on the wall before tea. _____

Creative Writing

Directions: Pretend you are a reporter for The Fairy Tale Times. What two questions would you ask Humpty Dumpty?

_____

- -

_____

- -

_____

- -

_____

- -

Name _____

Directions: Choose a word from the Word Bank to answer each crossword question. Write the answer in the correct word boxes.

Word Bank

women   horses   garden

many   egg   wall   army

ACROSS

1. Who put Humpty Dumpty together again?

3. Humpty Dumpty fell into the palace _____.

6. Humpty Dumpty's shell broke into _____ pieces.

DOWN

1. Humpty Dumpty fell off the _____.

2. Humpty Dumpty was an _____.

4. The King's _____ could not fix Humpty Dumpty.

5. The entire King's _____ could not fix Humpty Dumpty.

Name_____

Directions: Cut out the Humpty Dumpty puzzle pieces and glue him back together.

The Fairy Tale Times

Bruised but Happy —
Our New Princess!

After years of looking, the Prince has at last found his Princess!

"It's all thanks to my mother," said the Prince.

"A pretty woman asked for shelter during the storm. I did not know what to think. She said she was a real Princess, but it was hard tell. Many women might tell a lie, just to marry a prince."

For years, the Queen has wanted her son to get married. She also said that the Prince was too fussy. The Queen had a plan.

The royal maids took the sheets off the guest room bed. A small pea was put on the mattress. Then another 20 mattresses were put on the bed. Finally, a ladder was put next to the bed.

The Princess was then brought to the guest room. She climbed up the ladder and went to sleep.

The Prince told us, "the next morning the poor girl could not walk. She was all black and blue—from one little pea! Such soft skin could only belong to a real Princess."

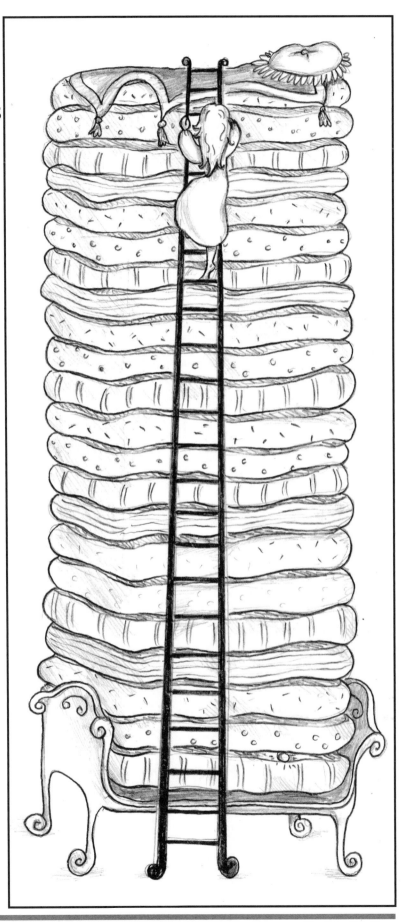

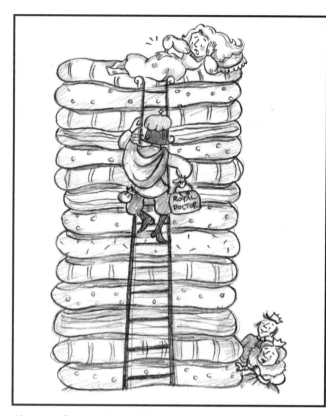

"We knew then," said the Queen, "that we had found a real princess! We found the girl who would marry my son!"

The Princess was unable to speak to us today. She is still in a lot of pain. The Royal Doctor says he has never seen anything like it.

A maid in the Palace was fired today for talking to The Fairy Tale Times. She said she found two cans of paint in the guestroom.

"One was black and one was blue. If those bruises are real, I am a talking monkey," said the maid.

The Queen said it was best that the maid left. "Talking monkeys are not fit to make the bed for a real Princess."

The wedding will take place next week.

Name _____

Directions: Write an answer to the following question.

Why do you think the maid was told to leave the palace?

Directions: Circle **yes** or **no** for each sentence.

1. It was a sunny morning when the princess
    asked for shelter.   **yes**   **no**

2. There were 30 mattresses on the bed.   **yes**   **no**

3. The doctor never came to see the bruised Princess.   **yes**   **no**

4. The wedding will take place in one week.   **yes**   **no**

5. The Princess climbed up a ladder to get into bed.   **yes**   **no**

6. A maid found two pots of paint.   **yes**   **no**

Name_____

Directions: Look at the pictures at the bottom of the page.
Cut them out along the dotted lines and glue them in the correct order.

1	2
3	4

Name ______________________________

Creative Art

Directions: Create the Princess's quilt. Draw a different design in each square.

Word Search

Directions: Circle the words from the Word Bank in the word search.
The words may be horizontal or vertical.

t	j	k	v	p	a	l	a	c	e	q
m	a	p	z	r	x	r	y	n	x	l
w	e	d	d	i	n	g	u	m	z	a
o	t	n	z	n	x	l	n	d	c	d
p	r	i	n	c	e	x	w	e	h	d
e	f	v	o	e	j	b	x	g	x	e
a	c	t	p	s	h	e	l	t	e	r
c	r	k	z	s	x	d	y	u	k	w

Word Bank

palace
prince
princess
wedding
pea
bed
shelter
ladder

The Fairy Tale Times

The Big Sleep is Over!

After 100 years, Sleeping Beauty has woken up!

The thick, thorny branches hiding the Palace are gone. The evil spell cast by the Wicked Fairy has been broken. Sleeping Beauty's big sleep was ended by the kiss of a Prince.

"We are all thrilled!" said the King. He was still in his pajamas, but looked very happy. "Now we can get on with our lives. It is a great feeling," said the King.

The King said he was sorry, but everyone will have to wait. "The women are too busy washing their hair. A hundred years is a long time to go without a mirror. It may be a while before they are ready to come out."

The Prince stood next to the King outside the Palace. The Prince said, "Ever since I was a boy, I have wanted to wake up Sleeping Beauty. Now my dream has come true!"

The whole country wants to see Sleeping Beauty and the Queen. For two days a large crowd has been waiting. Sadly, both the women will not leave the Palace.

"It will be nice to get to know Sleeping Beauty better," said the Prince. "I have not seen her since she has woken up. She has been very busy. She has to catch up on the latest fashions. She needs to eat a lot. A hundred years is a very long time to go without food. But I am not in a hurry. I can wait."

Let's hope he does not have to wait another hundred years!

Fairy Tale Times Drawing Contest

Draw a picture of what you think Sleeping Beauty will look like today.

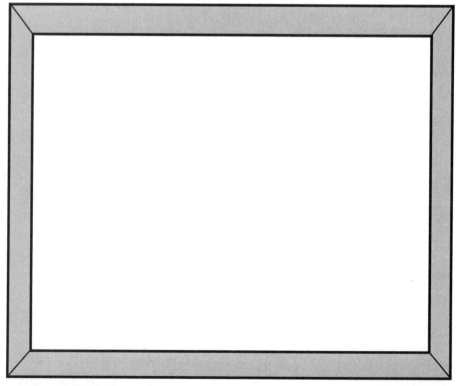

Name_____

Directions: A **fact** is something that is true. An **opinion** is something that a person thinks, believes, or feels. Write the word "**fact**" or the word "**opinion**" next to each sentence.

_____ 1. Sleeping Beauty was asleep for 100 years.

_____ 2. Sleeping Beauty is very messy.

_____ 3. A large crowd has been waiting for 2 days to see Sleeping Beauty and the Queen.

_____ 4. Since the Prince had been a small boy, he had dreamed of waking Sleeping Beauty.

_____ 5. Sleeping Beauty will look better when she learns about the latest fashions.

Creative Writing

Directions: Pretend you are a reporter for *The Fairy Tale Times*. What two questions would you ask Sleeping Beauty?

_____

_ _

_____

_____

_ _

_____

_____

_ _

_____

Name _____

Directions: Hide the palace by drawing lots of thick, thorny branches all over the palace walls.

Directions: Choose the correct word from the Word Bank to complete each sentence.

Word Bank:	branches	spell	happy	eat	dream	wash

1. The Prince was _____ when Sleeping Beauty woke up.

2. The evil _____ was cast by the Wicked Fairy!

3. Sleeping Beauty needs to _____ a lot of food.

4. The Prince said, "My _____ has come true!"

5. Thorny _____ were hiding the palace.

6. Sleeping Beauty wanted to _____ her hair before seeing the people.

Name _____

Directions: The **main idea** tells what the story is about. Read the following sentences and circle the sentence that you think best explains the main idea of the story.

1. Sleeping Beauty will learn about new fashions and she will eat a lot of food.

2. After 100 years Sleeping Beauty has woken up when the Prince's kiss broke the evil spell!

3. The King and Queen are excited that the Prince and Sleeping Beauty will be married.

Directions: **Antonyms** are two different words that have the opposite meaning. For example, "hot" and "cold" would be antonyms. Draw a line from each word in **Column A** to its matching antonym in **Column B**.

Column A	Column B
long	dirty
beautiful	happy
asleep	ugly
clean	girl
boy	short
sad	awake

Fastest Young Hare on the Block Beaten by Old Tortoise!

It was the biggest upset in animal sports history. Tom Terrantino, an eighty-year-old tortoise, won the one-mile race!

Before the race, people said it was cruel to let an old tortoise race against the fast four year-old hare. The hare, Henry Highlegs, has run many races. No one had ever beaten him.

Tom spoke to The Fairy Tale Times after the race. Tom was asked how it felt to be the oldest animal ever to win the one-mile race.

He said, "Stop calling me old. I am not even middle-aged! Did you know that tortoises can live to be 200 years old? Henry Highlegs might only be four, but he will be lucky if he makes it to ten. He is the one you should be calling old, not me!"

"I am sorry Tom, but you are kind of slow," the reporter said. "Tell us, how did you do it? How did you beat Henry?"

Tom replied, "Slow and steady. Slow and steady wins the race!"

It sure did for Tom! When asked if he had thought about trying any other sports? Tom said, "Well, I thought I would like to try the high jump, but my shell is kind of heavy. It might hold me back. Maybe I could try swimming or even boxing. But right now I want to rest. I am a little tired."

Henry Highlegs would not talk to The Fairy Tale Times. In fact, no one has seen him since his mad dash to the finish line.

Reporters did get to speak to his good friend, Lenny Longlegs. Without Lenny, Henry would not have made it to the finish line at all. Lenny found Henry fast asleep along the side of the road.

"Poor Henry. This will take him a long time to get over," Lenny said. "It's a shame. Henry only wanted to give Tom a head start. Henry faked being asleep, so he would not win by such a long way. What can I say? While he was faking being asleep — Henry really did fall asleep!"

The crowd left Tom Tarrantino waiting at the track for his family. He had hoped his wife and two sons would make it to the race. There was still no sign of them when we left.

Name

Directions: Look at the pictures at the bottom of the page.
Cut them out along the dotted lines and glue them in the correct order.

1	2
3	4

Name_____

Directions: Choose a word from the Word Bank to answer each crossword question. Write the answer in the correct word boxes.

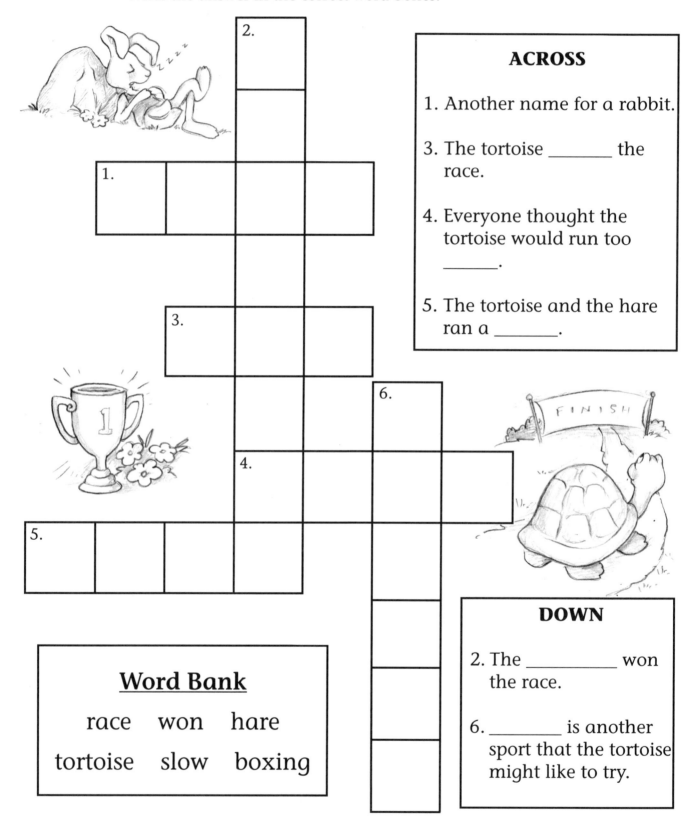

ACROSS

1. Another name for a rabbit.

3. The tortoise _____ the race.

4. Everyone thought the tortoise would run too _____.

5. The tortoise and the hare ran a _____.

DOWN

2. The _____ won the race.

6. _____ is another sport that the tortoise might like to try.

Word Bank

race   won   hare

tortoise   slow   boxing

Name_____

Directions: Read the words at the bottom of the page. Which words describe the tortoise? Which words describe the hare? Which words can be used to describe both of the animals. Cut out the word boxes along the dotted lines and glue them into the correct section of the Venn diagram.

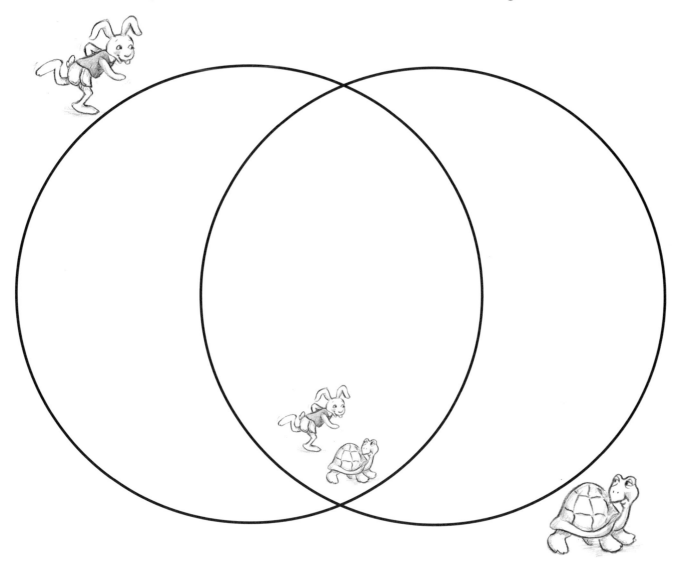

fast	soft	ran in a race	lost the race
slow	hard	won the race	likes to run

The Fairy Tale Times

Fairy Godmother Hits Out at Cinderella!

Read it here first! The Fairy Godmother tells all to The Fairy Tale Times.

The Fairy Godmother and Cinderella are not talking. Both women are angry! Both women have hurt feelings!

"After all I did for that girl! She did not invite me to the wedding! If it was not for me, she would still be in rags! She would still be sweeping and mopping floors!" said the Fairy Godmother.

Last year, the Fairy Godmother helped the poor girl. She used some special magic.

She turned a pumpkin into a coach. She turned seven mice into horses. And she made a new dress and glass slippers for Cinderella. The Fairy Godmother did all this so Cinderella could go to the ball.

At the ball, Cinderella lost one of her glass slippers. The Prince found it.

This was the slipper that helped the Prince learn where she lived.

And, as all our readers know . . . they fell in love and planned their wedding.

The wedding invitations were mailed. The Fairy Godmother did not get one. She was very upset.

Things got even worse. Two days before the wedding, Cinderella saw the Fairy Godmother in town! They both turned away. No one even tried to talk.

Later, Cinderella went to the Fairy Godmother's house. She tried to talk to her. But the old Fairy would not even open her door.

Cinderella has asked The Fairy Tale Times to print this letter. We hope the Fairy Godmother will read it.

Dear Fairy Godmother,

I have just found out the truth. My wicked stepmother and stepsisters still do not want me to be happy. They told the Palace Postman not to bring you the invitation. They paid him a lot of money to throw it away.

They wanted you to get angry. They hoped you would cast a bad spell on me. I did not know that you did not get an invitation. I was upset when you were not at the wedding. I do want to talk to you. I am so sorry.

If you read this message, please, please come and see me. I wept when you did not come to the wedding.

With best wishes,
Princess Cinderella

P.S. Please feel free to do something nasty to my stepmother and stepsisters.

All we can do now is hope the Fairy Godmother reads The Fairy Tale Times!

Name_____

Directions: A **cause** tells why something has happened and an **effect** tells what happened. Draw a line from each cause in **Column A** to its matching effect in **Column B**.

Column A   ## Column B

1. The Fairy Godmother gave Cinderella a new dress,

2. The Fairy Godmother did not get a wedding invitation to Cinderella's wedding,

3. Cinderella wrote a message to the Fairy Godmother,

4. The stepmother paid the postman money not to deliver the invitation to the Fairy Godmother,

a. so she would think that Cinderella did not want her at the wedding.

b. which hurt her feelings.

c. so she could go to the ball.

d. in hopes that the Fairy Godmother would read it and forgive her.

Comprehension

Directions: Read each question. Circle the picture that answers each question.

1. How did Cinderella get to the ball?

3. How did Cinderella apologize to the Fairy Godmother?

2. What fell off Cinderella's foot?

4. What did Cinderella and the Prince do?

Directions: Circle the words from the Word Bank in the word search.
The words may be horizontal or vertical.

```
f  x  b  c  w  y  p  s  q
a  x  s  i  s  t  e  r  s
i  q  c  n  t  v  d  x  l
r  a  g  d  a  n  c  e  i
y  s  m  e  u  x  g  k  p
c  d  f  r  m  a  i  l  p
n  m  w  e  p  y  x  o  e
b  a  l  l  q  w  x  v  r
j  q  g  l  a  s  s  e  s
s  e  e  a  w  n  f  z  o
```

Word Bank: sisters fairy dance see
slippers Cinderella glass mail ball love

Name _____

Directions: Look at each of the pictures. Then write a sentence about what you think is happening next to each of the pictures.

The Fairy Tale Times

Rapunzel—Missing for 18 Years is Alive and Well!

18 years ago The Fairy Tale Times told the sad story of an only child stolen from her parents. We tried to help find the lost girl, but thought she would never be seen again.

We can now report that the parents have spoken to their daughter. She is alive and well, and living with her royal husband in the mountains!

The parents were excited to tell their daughter's amazing story.

"We could not believe it!" said Derek, Rapunzel's father. "She has spent most of her life locked in a tower. That old witch was her only visitor."

"The witch would climb up Rapunzel's hair to get in through the window," said June, Rapunzel's mother, still angry with the witch. "Mind you, she must be like me. I've always had strong hair, haven't I Derek?"

"Indeed you have June. I swear, if ever I get my hands on that witch, I'm going to climb up her hair, and see how she likes it!" said Derek.

"But then — this is where it gets romantic," smiled June, "A Prince walked by the tower and heard Rapunzel singing. He fell in love with her lovely voice. I have always had a lovely voice, haven't I Derek?" asked June.

"Indeed you have, June. And then the Prince pretended to be the witch. He climbed up her hair. They talked, and she fell in love too."

"But then Rapunzel did something a bit daft. I am afraid she got that from her dad — you're a bit daft sometimes, aren't you Derek?" said June.

"Indeed I am June. Please get on with the story, we haven't got all day. We have a long journey ahead of us." said Derek.

"Well, Rapunzel let it slip how much heavier the witch is hanging off her hair than the Prince! Can you believe it? So then the witch cut off all Rapunzel's hair, and threw her out of the tower!"

"But she's a cunning old witch," said Derek, "When the Prince came that night, she held down Rapunzel's hair for him to climb up. Fancy coming face to face with that old hag when he was expecting to see our lovely daughter," added Derek.

"Then the witch threw the Prince out the tower. His eyes were hurt so badly that he couldn't see any more. My eyes aren't as good as they were, are they Derek?"

"No June. So they both wandered around for months! No food, no money, and not knowing where the other one was," added Derek.

"Finally, the Prince heard Rapunzel singing. And this is the best part — it's so romantic. They hug each other and Rapunzel cries. (I've always loved a good cry, haven't I Derek?) A few of her tears drop into his eyes and help him to see again. Isn't that the loveliest thing you ever heard?" asked June.

The Fairy Tale Times is happy to report that there are still some happy endings. We also warn our readers not to climb up anyone's hair.

Name_____

Directions: Read the question in each box. Write your answer in each speech bubble.

1. What do you think Rapunzel is saying to the witch?

2. What do you think the Prince is saying to the witch?

3. What do you think Rapunzel is saying to the Prince?

4. What do you think Rapunzel's parents are saying to her?

Name_____

Directions: Look at each of the characters. Then write a list of words that would describe each of them.

Rapunzel	Witch	Prince

Name_____

Directions: Choose the correct word from the Word Bank to complete each sentence.

Word Bank: found   climb   cut   tower   locked   singing

1. Rapunzel has been _____ alive and well!

2. Rapunzel has been _____ in a tower!

3. The Witch would _____ up Rapunzel's hair!

4. The Prince walked by and heard Rapunzel _____ .

5. The Witch threw the prince out of the _____ .

6. The Witch _____ off all of Rapunzel's hair!

Directions: A **cause** tells why something has happened and an **effect** tells what happened. Draw a line from each cause in **Column A** to its matching effect in **Column B**.

Column A

1. Rapunzel was stolen as a baby,

2. Rapunzel told the Witch she was heavier than the Prince,

3. The Witch threw the Prince out of the tower,

4. The Prince finally heard Rapunzel singing,

Column B

a. which made the Witch angry.

b. so they were able to find each other.

c. and grew up locked in a tower.

d. which hurt his eyes.

The Fairy Tale Times

King Naked!
Or Are We All Fools!

Sunday, May 3rd

No one knows what to think after yesterday's royal parade. We had all heard about the King's new robes that were made from fine gold and smooth silk. They were going to be stunning. They were also going to be invisible — if you can believe that.

Yesterday, when the King walked through the streets, all our hearts sank. The Ministers held the royal train and admired the robes that we could not see.

Then came the moment we will never forget. Jack Cant, a scruffy boy of ten, shouted, ***"The King is buck-naked!"***

The crowd went wild, but the parade carried on all the way through the town. Today, the King and his Ministers are locked in the Palace. They will not speak to the press.

Monday, May 4th

The King's Minister calls the people fools! 48 hours later, Minister Gert Wump, the King's closest aide, came out of the Palace to answer our questions.

"Mr. Wump, if the King was naked (which he was), he is a fool, and you, his Ministers, are fools. What do you have to say to that?" asked one of the reporters.

The Minister smiled a nasty smile, and said, "You must realize that the King was not naked. It is the people of this land who are the fools. It is a good thing that you have a wise King and clever Ministers to look after you foolish people."

The Fairy Tale Times reporter asked Minister Wump, "When will we see the King?"

"Tomorrow," the Minister snapped.

Tuesday, May 5th

Three days after his parade, the King finally came out of the Palace. He was alone and wearing an old dressing gown. His hair was a mess, like a white bird's nest. He shouted to the huge crowd outside the Palace.

"Greetings, my people. Over the last three days, I have spent a lot of time thinking instead of looking in a mirror. I have thought long and hard. On the one hand, I have thought that the people of my land might all be fools. On the other hand, I have thought, I am the fool and not fit to be your King."

"Today, I found out which was true. I went to my Ministers, wearing my new robes and asked them how I looked," said the King. "Stunning," said one. "Lovely," said another. "Shiny," and "Flowing." "Like the sun," said another.

"And when I asked them if the robes made my tummy look big, they all shouted, 'No,' your Majesty."

So the King asked the Ministers one more time. "Do you really like my robes?" All the Ministers said, "Yes!"

"Well, very good," said the King, smiling for the first time in three days. "You will all be glad to know there is lots of this magic cloth left. Lots and lots of it! You will take off your dull, ugly clothes. You will wrap this lovely magic cloth around you, and you will come outside with me and speak to the people. Then they will have to believe us."

"Not one of them was willing to look like a fool like me. So now I know the truth. I am sorry. I was naked," confessed the King.

The King ended his speech by saying, "I have been a vain King. I have wasted time and money on my clothes. I should have been looking after you. If you forgive me, I promise to be a better King."

There was silence. Then someone started to clap. It was Jack Cant's father. Soon, the whole crowd was clapping and cheering the King. He waved back and looked more like a true King in his old dressing gown than he ever looked in his fine new robes.

Name _____

Directions: Read each sentence about the story. Write a "**T**" on the blank if the
sentence is true. Write an "**F**" on the blank if the sentence is false.

1. When the King marched in the parade he really
    was naked.   _____

2. The little boy who yelled, "the King is buck-naked,"
    was named Georgie Porgie.   _____

3. On Monday, May 4, Minister Wump called the people fools.   _____

4. On Tuesday, May 5, the King came out in an old
    dressing gown and told the people he was sorry.   _____

5. All the Ministers wanted to wear invisible clothes too!   _____

6. The King promised to change his ways and become a
    better king.   _____

Creative Writing

Directions: Draw a picture of Jack Cant and write a sentence about him.

Name_____

Directions: Look at the pictures at the bottom of the page.
Cut them out along the dotted lines and glue them in the correct order.

1	**2**
3	**4**

Name_____

Directions: Pretend you are a reporter for *The Fairy Tale Times.*
What two questions would you ask the King?

_____

- -

_____

_____

- -

_____

_____

- -

_____

_____

- -

_____

Directions: Design a real royal robe for the King to wear.

High-Frequency, Easy-to-Sound Out, and Special Words for Each Story

a	bird's	ended	going	is	maid	open	see
about	bit	enough	gold	it	maids	other	seen
added	black	even	gone	it's	mail	our	set
after	blue	ever	good	jump	mailed	out	seven
again	both	everyone	got	jumped	make	outside	she
against	bring	eyes	great	just	makes	over	sheets
ago	brought	face	grips	keep	man	own	shell
aide	boy	fact	had	kind	many	pain	should
alive	busy	fail	hag	king	may	paint	shouted
all	but	faked	hair	king's	maybe	parents	side
alone	by	faking	hairs	kiss	me	part	sign
along	calling	fall	hand	kissed	men	pea	silly
also	calls	fallen	hands	kissing	mending	people	since
am	came	family	hanging	knew	mess	pieces	sing
an	can	fast	happy	know	mice	pig	singing
and	cans	fastest	hard	knowing	might	pigs	sit
animal	cast	father	hare	ladder	mile	place	skin
another	chair	fear	has	land	mind	plan	sleep
answer	children	feel	have	large	missed	planned	sleeping
any	child	feeling	haven't	last	missing	please	sleeps
anyone	clap	fell	he	later	moment	poor	slept
anything	clean	felt	head	learn	money	press	slip
are	climb	few	heard	leave	months	pretty	slow
aren't	climbed	finally	hearts	left	mopping	print	small
around	cloth	find	heavy	let	more	promise	smile
as	come	finish	held	lets	morning	pumpkin	smiled
asked	coming	fired	help	letter	most	put	snapped
asleep	could	first	helped	like	mother	queen	so
at	couldn't	fit	her	likes	must	queen's	soft
away	cries	fix	hiding	line	my	questions	some
back	cry	floors	high	little	nasty	race	something
bad	cut	food	him	live	needs	races	son
badly	dad	fool	his	lived	nest	rags	son's
ball	dash	fools	hits	lives	never	read	sorry
be	daughter	for	hold	living	new	readers	speak
bear	daughter's	forget	home	lock	next	real	spell
beaten	day	found	hope	locked	nice	really	spent
beauty	days	free	house	long	night	rest	spoke
been	did	friendly	horses	look	no	right	sport
bed	do	frog	how	looked	noon	road	start
before	door	from	hug	lost	not	robes	started
being	down	fussy	huge	lot	now	room	steady
believe	dress	garden	hurt	love	of	run	still
belong	dull	get	I	loved	off	sad	stop
best	during	girl	if	lovely	old	sadly	stopped
better	easy	give	I'm	lucky	oldest	said	stood
big	eat	glad	in	mad	on	sank	stores
bigger	eaten	glass	indeed	made	one	saw	story
biggest	egg	go	into	magic	only	say	streets

strong
sure
sun
sweep
sweeping
such
take
talk
talking
tears
tell
tells
ten
than
thanks
that
the
their
them
then
there
they
thick
thing
think
tired
this
those
thought
three
threw
thrilled
through
throw
time
tiny
to
today
together
told
tomorrow
too
took
town
track
train
trick
tried
true
trust

truth
try
tummy
turn
turned
two
ugly
up
upset
upstairs
us
used
vain
very
wandered
wait
waiting
wake
walk
walked
wall
want
wanted
wants
warn
was
washing
wave
way
we
wearing
week
well
went
were
what
when
where
which
white
who
whole
wicked
wife
wild
will
win
wins
window
wise

wishes
with
without
woken
woman
women
won
woods
worked
would
wrap
years
yes
yesterday
you
young
your
you're

Special Words for Each Story

Special Words for Story #1
blow
brick
brothers
doctors
hospital
huffing
Paul
puffing
sticks
straw
visits
wolf

Special Words for Story #2
bottom
broken
Fairy Tale
Times
golden
human
Mr.
Mrs.
police
porridge

Special Words for Story #3
booth
events
fever
Fred
golden
handsome
husband
police
prince
princess
ribbit
scary

Special Words for Story #4
army
Humpty Dumpty
hooves
hundreds
palace
soldier
stomped
tea

Special Words for Story #5
bruised
guestroom
marry
mattress
mattresses
monkey
royal
shelter
storm
unable
wedding

Special Words for Story #6
branches
country
crowd
dream
evil
fashion
hundred
mirror
pajamas
thorny

Special Words for Story #7
cruel
earth
Henry Highlegs
history
Lenny Longlegs
middle-aged
replied
swimming
Tom Tarrantino
tortoise

Special Words for Story #8
angry
Cinderella
coach
Fairy Godmother
invite
invitations
marriage
message
midnight
misery
postman
slippers
stepmother
stepsisters
worse

Special Words for Story #9
amazing
daft
excited
expecting
journey
mountains
pretended
Rapunzel
report
romantic
royal
stolen
tower
voice
witch

Special Words for Story #10
admired
apology
buck-naked
cheering
clever
confessed
foolish
invisible
Jack Cant
Majesty
Ministers
Mr. Wert Gump
parade
scruffy
smooth silk
speech
stunning

Answer Key

Top of page 6
1. hospital; 2. bricks; 3. week;
4. huffing and puffing; 5. *answers will vary*

Bottom of page 6
Check students' work

Page 7
1. Wolf is blowing on the brick house.
2. The ambulance takes the wolf away.
3. The pigs are racing to get bricks at the Brick Warehouse.
4. The Wolf is in the hospital.

Page 10
Check students' work

Top of page 11
1. porridge; 2. chair; 3. hairs;
4. talk; 5. mess; 6. woods

Bottom of page 11
Check students' work

Page 14
Check students' work

Page 15
Check students' work

Page 16
Check students' work

Top of page 19
1. F; 2. T; 3. T; 4. F; 5. F; 6. T

Bottom of page 19
1. *check students' work*

Page 20
Across: 1. women; 3. garden; 6. many
Down: 1. wall; 2. egg; 4. horses; 5. army

Bottom of page 21
Check students' work

Top of page 25
Check students' work

Bottom of page 25
1. no; 2; no; 3. no;
4. yes; 5. yes 6. no

Page 26
1. The Princess asks for shelter from the storm.
2. The Queen puts a pea under the mattresses.
3. The Princess climbs up the ladder to get into bed.
4. The Princess wakes up sore and bruised.

Top of page 27
Check students' work

Bottom of page 27

t	j	k	v	p	a	l	a	c	e	q
m	a	p	z	r	x	r	y	n	x	l
w	e	d	d	i	n	g	u	m	z	a
o	t	n	z	n	x	l	n	d	c	d
p	r	i	n	c	e	x	w	e	h	d
e	f	v	o	e	j	b	x	g	x	e
a	c	t	p	s	h	e	l	t	e	r
c	r	k	z	s	x	d	y	u	k	w

Top of page 31
1. fact; 2. opinion; 3. fact; 4. fact; 5. opinion

Bottom of page 31
1. *check students' work*

Page 32
1. happy; 2. spell; 3. eat;
4. dream; 5. branches: 6. wash

Top of page 33
2. Sleeping Beauty has woken up when the Prince's kiss broke the evil spell.

Bottom of page 33
long/short; beautiful/ugly; asleep/awake;
clean/dirty; boy/girl; sad/happy

Page 37
1. The hare and the tortoise begin running the race.
2. The hare falls alseep.
3. The tortoise crosses the finish line.
4. The tortoise is given a trophy.

Answer Key

Page 38

> *Across:* 1. hare; 3. won; 4. slow; 5. race
> *Down:* 2. tortoise; 6. boxing

Page 38

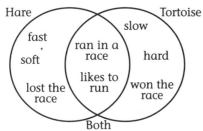

Top of page 44

> 1. c; 2. b; 3. d; 4. a

Bottom of page 44

> 1. pumpkin coach; 2. glass slipper
> 3. letter in newspaper 4. got married

Page 45

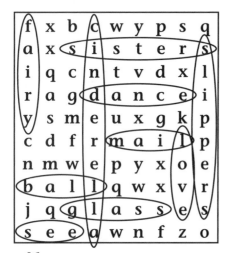

Page 46

> *Check students' work*

Page 51

> *Check students' work*

Top of page 53

> 1. found; 2. locked; 3. climb;
> 4. singing; 5. tower; 6. cut

Bottom of page 53

> 1. c; 2. a; 3. d; 4. b

Top of page 58

> 1. T; 2. F; 3. T; 4. T; 5. F; 6. T

Bottom of page 58

> *Check students' work*

Page 59

> 1. The people are shocked that the king is naked.
> 2. Jack Cant yells, "The King is buck-naked!"
> 3. Minister Gump stand in the palace and calls the people "fools."
> 4. The King aplogizes to the people.

Top of page 60

> *Check students' work*

Bottom of page 60

> *Check students' work*